BEYOND THE PERCENTILE

A FAMILY'S JOURNEY THROUGH JEE, FAILURES, AND FAITH

CHANDAN GOYAL

Made with ♥ on the Notion Press Platform
www.notionpress.com

Dedicated to all JEE and NEET aspirants and their parents—

To the students who brave sleepless nights, silent pressures, and endless doubts in pursuit of their dreams.

And to the parents who walk every step of the journey with unseen sacrifices, unshakable faith, and unconditional love.

Contents

Foreword — *vii*

Preface — *ix*

Acknowledgements — *xi*

Prologue — *xiii*

About the Author — *xv*

1. The Many Dreams Of An Eight-Year-Old — 1

2. Evenings Of Guidance, Echoes Of Dreams — 4

3. Lockdown Leisure And The Push Forward — 7

4. The Car Boot And Cardboard Box — 9

5. Shared Rides And Silent Bonds — 11

6. Kul Devi And Conversations Of The Soul — 13

7. Signs Of A Journey — 15

8. The Banner That Didn't Have His Name — 17

9. The One Who Set The Standards — 19

10. The First Setback — 21

11. Cracks Beneath The Numbers — 23

12. The Strength Named Bhawna — 26

13. Little Joys, Big Smiles — 29

14. Crisis Mode — 32

15. The Crossroads Of Confidence — 36

16. Trophies And Truths — 39

17. Footsteps And Feelings — 41

18. Health Vs. Hope — 44

19. IBBI Time – Struggles Beyond The Classroom — 46

Contents

20. Joy In Small Packets   49

21. Inertia Of Motion, Instincts & Intensive Planning 52

22. New Year, Same Grit   56

23. Rohan Saab – Dosti Wala Timeout   58

24. The Form, The Test, And The Silence   60

25. 28th January – First Attempt   63

26. When The Clouds Hovered Low   66

27. Ram Payari - Our Silent Companion   69

28. Turmeric Milk, Mornings, And Dreams   72

29. The Calm Before The Second Storm   74

30. The Second Attempt   76

31. The Calm After The Storm   79

32. The Silence Before The Next Sunrise   81

Growth Beyond Results   85

Lessons Beyond the Rank   87

Let the Journey Speak   91

Foreword

Every exam is more than just a test of knowledge—it's a test of character, of resilience, and of the bonds that hold a family together. When our son, Yojan, began his journey of JEE preparation, we, as parents, unknowingly enrolled ourselves in a parallel journey—of hope, fear, patience, and perseverance.

This book is not just a chronicle of preparation strategies or academic struggles. It is a reflection of emotions, of long nights filled with self-doubt, of early mornings starting with turmeric milk and hopeful prayers. It's about a boy who faced pressure that would shake the strongest of minds, and a family that stood by him like a wall of quiet strength.

Through ups and downs, success and silence, what emerged was not just a result, but a story. A story of how dreams sometimes change, how priorities realign, and how success is often more about the journey than the destination.

We hope this book offers comfort, guidance, and strength to every student and parent navigating a similar path. Whether your destination is an IIT, a medical college, or something else entirely—may you walk your road with courage, compassion, and clarity.

Let this story remind you: the effort is never wasted.

— Bhawna

Preface

This book was born from the heart—written not as an expert's guide to cracking competitive exams, but as a lived journey of a family navigating the emotional and academic rollercoaster of JEE preparation.

When my son, Yojan, began preparing for one of the most competitive exams in India, we, like countless other families, stepped into a world of expectations, sacrifices, routines, and uncertainties. What unfolded over the next two years was not just a study plan but a life lesson—on handling pressure, managing failure, staying hopeful, and above all, supporting each other when things didn't go as planned.

Through late-night discussions, morning head massages, last-minute revisions, and silent prayers, we saw the real test wasn't just academic—it was emotional. It tested relationships, patience, and the definition of success.

This book follows our journey—not as a how-to manual, but as a story. A story of effort, of slipping and standing again, of learning even when outcomes weren't favorable. A story for students who are trying their best, and parents who are silently walking alongside.

If this book brings comfort to even one aspirant who feels overwhelmed, or helps a parent understand their child a little better, it will have served its purpose.

This is our story. Perhaps it's yours too.

— Chandan Goyal

Acknowledgements

This book is not just a reflection of our journey—it is a tapestry woven with the love, support, and strength of many people who stood by us during some of the most challenging and meaningful years of our lives.

First and foremost, I thank Yojan, whose perseverance, honesty, and emotional strength through this demanding phase became the soul of this story. His courage to rise after each fall and his ability to smile even in pressure taught me more than any book ever could.

To Bhawna, my wife and Yojan's guiding star—your unwavering commitment, selfless support, and quiet sacrifices turned obstacles into stepping stones. Your role went far beyond being a mother; you were a mentor, a teacher, a friend, and a silent warrior.

My heartfelt thanks to my parents, whose blessings, unconditional love, and presence kept our home a place of strength and calm. Dadu's daily head massages and comforting words were more therapeutic than any medicine.

Special thanks to Krishna, Rohan, and all of Yojan's friends who walked parts of this journey with him. And to all the teachers, mentors, and well-wishers who played a role—however big or small—in shaping this path.

This book is for every student who's given their best, and every parent who's stood silently behind them, wiping tears and whispering encouragement.

With deepest gratitude,
Chandan Goyal

Prologue

Every parent dreams of seeing their child succeed, but the journey to that success is often riddled with challenges, moments of doubt, and the desire to shield them from the burdens of life. This book is not just about an academic pursuit; it is about the journey of growth, perseverance, and learning—both for the child and for the parent.

As I sat by Yojan's side, watching him face the pressures of the JEE exam, I realized that it wasn't just about cracking the code of equations or mastering formulas. It was about learning to navigate life itself—how to cope with failures, how to rise after a fall, and how to maintain your spirit even when everything around you seems to be falling apart.

The world of JEE preparation is a realm filled with endless nights, sleepless mornings, and the constant pressure of performance. But beyond that, it's about learning to find balance, to deal with stress, and to recognize that the real victory lies not in the rank, but in the strength of character you build along the way.

This book is a glimpse into our family's journey through the highs and lows of the JEE preparation saga. It's about my son, Yojan's dreams and struggles, my wife Bhawna's relentless support, and the constant emotional and mental turmoil we faced as parents. It is about the sacrifices made, the battles fought—both visible and invisible—and the immense learning that comes from trying, failing, and trying again.

Above all, this is a story about growth—not just academic, but personal. In the end, success isn't measured by a number on a paper. It's measured by how much you've grown as an individual, how much you've learned about yourself, and how much you're willing to give back to the world once you've reached your destination.

I invite you, dear reader, to walk with us through this journey. Whether you're a student preparing for exams, a parent walking the same path, or someone who has been through similar challenges, this story will resonate with you. It is a reminder that no matter the outcome, every step forward is a victory in itself.

About The Author

Chandan Goyal is an Industrial Engineer with years of experience in both industry and teaching. He has a deep passion for mentoring students and has witnessed firsthand the challenges of academic preparation. In his free time, he enjoys writing, reflecting on life's lessons, and spending time with his family.

CHAPTER ONE

The Many Dreams of an Eight-Year-Old

The afternoon sun was soft that day, filtering in through the curtains, casting golden patterns on the living room floor. Bhawna was in the kitchen, arranging the last of the snacks on a tray, while I fluffed up the cushions on the sofa—our home buzzing with a quiet excitement.

"Ji, did you check if the tea's ready?" Bhawna called out.

"Yeah, it's brewing. Strong, just how Ashok bhaiya likes it."

Within minutes, the doorbell rang.

I opened the door to find my cousin Dr. Ashok standing there, his usual warm smile lighting up his face.

"Bhaiya!" I welcomed him with a hug. "So good to see you!"

"Same here, Chandan! It's been too long," he said, stepping in and looking around. "And your house looks as lively as ever."

Bhawna joined us, wiping her hands on her dupatta. "Namaste, bhaiya. You're right on time. Snacks are ready!"

She handed him a cup of tea and a plate full of mathri and paneer pakoras. We all settled into the living room, catching up on family news, health, work—everything under the sun.

Suddenly, Dr. Ashok looked around and asked, "Where's the little one? Where's Yojan?"

"He's in his room," Bhawna smiled. "Probably building some Lego skyscraper."

I called out, "Yojan beta, come here! Ashok tau ji is here!"

In a few seconds, Yojan trotted in, eyes bright, cheeks a bit red from excitement—or maybe from running.

"Namaste, tau ji!" he said, doing a quick little bow with folded hands.

Dr. Ashok chuckled and pulled him close. "Arre wah! You've grown taller, haven't you? Tell me, young man, what do you want to be when you grow up?"

Yojan didn't even blink. With a puffed chest and a sparkle in his eyes, he replied, "Prime Minister of India!"

There was a short silence, followed by loud laughter from all of us.

"Wah, wah!" Ashok bhaiya clapped. "Ambitious! I like that."

I just looked at Yojan in amusement, impressed by the conviction in his voice.

Later that night, when the house was quieter and Bhawna was putting away the dishes, I sat beside Yojan while he was scribbling in his notebook.

"So... Prime Minister, huh?" I asked casually.

He grinned. "Yeah... but now I think I want to be like Messi."

I raised an eyebrow. "Football Messi?"

"Of course! I've been practicing in school. I scored two goals last week!"

I smiled, ruffled his hair, and said, "You'll be the next Messi then."

A few days later, we were walking to the park together. The sky was painted with evening hues, and I asked again, "So what's the latest aim?"

Yojan thought for a moment, then said seriously, "IAS officer."

I stopped walking and looked at him. "That's a big one."

He nodded. "I want to help people. Listened lot about IASs from mammu."

I couldn't help but laugh. "From PM to Messi to IAS... I wonder what next week will bring."

But deep inside, I was fascinated—not by the changing dreams, but by the spark that never faded. A fire was beginning to glow in that little heart, shaping a path he had yet to fully discover.

CHAPTER TWO

Evenings of Guidance, Echoes of Dreams

Jagraon isn't a big town. Here, people know each other, or at least know someone who knows you. Being an engineer by qualification but a Physics teacher by passion, I had built a name for myself teaching JEE and NEET aspirants for over two decades. Word spread easily. Every March or April, just as the academic year would begin to stir, parents would start appearing at my door.

It became a ritual—returning home around 7:30 p.m. after a day's work, only to find a few parents already waiting or arriving shortly after. Bhawna would give me a knowing smile and head to the kitchen, preparing tea and setting out snacks, while I settled down in the drawing room.

"Ji, aap baithiye. Main chai lati hoon," Bhawna would say, already busy with her tray.

One evening, as I entered the house, I saw three sets of slippers neatly lined up at the door. In the drawing room, two couples were already seated, sipping water. Yojan, still in his casual school clothes, quietly moved between the guests, offering them water and then disappearing into the kitchen to assist Bhawna.

"Sir, we want to know about the JEE coaching," one father began. "We've heard about the institute where you teach. But what about Aakash? Is it better?"

Another mother chimed in, "Expenses are also a concern. And how do we know our child is suitable for JEE or NEET?"

The questions were always the same—but the concern behind them was genuine. We spoke about study patterns, discipline, the importance of foundation building, and above all, the emotional support kids need.

Sometimes these discussions lasted an hour. Parents came with doubts and left with clarity—or at least, direction.

What many didn't notice was that Yojan, usually sitting silently on the staircase or in the adjacent room, was listening. His eyes observed every word I said, his ears caught every mention of IIT, NEET, careers, and dreams.

That night, after the guests had left and Bhawna was winding down the kitchen, I found Yojan lying on the floor with his legs up on the sofa, staring at the ceiling.

"Kya soch rahe ho?" I asked, sitting beside him.

He turned to me and smiled. "Papa, IIT tough hota hai na?"

"Bohot. But not impossible," I replied. "Why do you ask?"

"I was just thinking... JEE waale jo hote hain na... they seem smart. You speak so confidently about them."

I smiled. "You can be one of them too, if you want. But only if *you* want it."

He nodded slowly, still staring at the ceiling. "I think I want to. Not sure wh. And I like how you explain to those parents. Feels like something big."

I didn't say anything more. Just placed my hand on his head and let that quiet moment speak for itself. Maybe he hadn't made a decision yet. But something inside him had shifted—curiosity had sparked. And sometimes, that's where all great journeys begin.

CHAPTER THREE

Lockdown Leisure and the Push Forward

When the lockdown began, Yojan was in Class 8. Like everyone else, we were confined to our home, routines altered, the world outside suddenly on pause. Yojan, being the sincere student he was, continued to attend his online classes with full discipline. Sitting in front of the screen, camera on, homework done on time—he never gave us a reason to complain.

But once his classes were over, the long afternoons stretched endlessly. With little else to do, he started finding new interests. One such discovery was cooking.

Most afternoons, when Bhawna and I were resting after lunch, the clinking of utensils and the aroma of something frying would drift from the kitchen.

"Ji, Yojan fir se kitchen mein hai," Bhawna would say, half amused and half concerned.

"Let him try, Bhawna. He's learning something," I'd respond with a smile.

But the real task would begin after the cooking—cleaning up. The kitchen would often resemble a mini battlefield.

"Yojan!" Bhawna would call out. "Beta, tumne toh kitchen ko museum bana diya!"

"Sorry, Mumma," he'd grin, holding out a piece of cake or a slightly burnt paneer bhurji. "Taste toh kar lo."

Despite the mess, we tasted everything. Because every dish carried his effort, his curiosity, and his growing independence.

He also took up pencil sketching. For hours, he'd sit with his drawing pad, shading outlines of cricketers, animals, and even abstract shapes. The walls of his room slowly started collecting these works—some better than others, but all equally precious.

Yet, with so much time still in hand, I felt this was the right opportunity to push him a bit.

One evening, while we sat together on the veranda sipping tea, I said, "Yojan, why don't you start Class 9 Maths? You have time, and it'll give you a headstart."

He frowned a little, clearly not excited by the idea.

"But Papa, I'm still in 8th."

"I know, beta. But you're capable. You've always handled challenges well. This will help later when the real grind starts."

He didn't argue. He simply nodded and said, "Okay, I'll try."

And try he did. Even though it wasn't his favorite thing, he followed through—just because I asked him to. That obedience, that trust, always touched me. He didn't do it out of passion then—but perhaps a seed had been sown.

CHAPTER FOUR

The Car Boot and Cardboard Box

The day Class 10 board exams ended, a new energy ran through me. I was excited—not just because the results would be out soon, but because it was time. Time for Yojan to begin his JEE journey. With me.

He was going to join the same institute where I had been teaching for years. And I had already made up my mind to guide him personally, right from day one.

I stepped into the institute and headed straight to the storeroom, collecting a bundle of books—reference materials, test series, previous year questions—all the sample copies we had received from publishers over the years.

"Santosh!" I called out to our office assistant. "Le bhai, ye books le jaa. Gaadi ke boot mein rakh de."

He hurried over and took the stacks from my hands. As he stepped out, I heard him ask, "Sir, aapki car kahan khadi hai?"

"Chote Lal!" I called to our security guard, who was lounging on a plastic chair nearby. "Isse dikha de meri car kahan hai."

"Woh jo peepal ke neeche khadi hai, white waali i20," Chote Lal pointed. "Number plate PB 25 H 8888 hai."

I smiled and nodded, then turned back inside.

That evening, I began another small but satisfying project. "Bhawne, koi purana cardboard box pada hai kya?" I asked Bhawna, rummaging through the storeroom.

"Kyoon?" she looked at me curiously.

"Yojan ke liye car mein ek study table jaisa setup banana hai. Kabhi kabhi time mile toh woh wahan padhe."

She handed me a box that once carried rice packets. I pulled out a cutter, some tape, and leftover chart papers.

For the next hour, I was in full engineering mode—measuring, cutting, pasting. Yojan peeked in now and then, trying to make sense of the mess.

When I finally finished, I held it up like a trophy. "Dekho, perfect box! Yeh back seat mein rakhenge. On the way, reading kar sakta hai."

Bhawna laughed. "Bas, ab ispe patent le lo."

I grinned, more proud than she probably expected. It wasn't just a cardboard box. It was a beginning. A symbol. A father's quiet excitement for the journey ahead.

CHAPTER FIVE

Shared Rides and Silent Bonds

Classes started in the first week of April. Yojan and I began commuting together in the car. Almost every morning, it was the same drill.

"Beta, jaldi karo," I'd call out. "Tumhara bag aur bottle main gaadi mein rakh raha hoon."

Still buttoning his shirt or looking for his other sock, Yojan would shout back, "Coming, Papa!"

Most days, his shoes stayed in the car—he'd put them on during the ride, half awake, staring out the window.

His classes ended by 2 PM, but my office hours stretched till 6:30. So, he would wait in my vacant room at the academy. A bench became his afternoon resting spot. Sometimes I'd peek in and find him curled up, dozing off, using his bag as a pillow.

Other times, he'd quietly wander through the institute, looking for me—not always with doubts, sometimes just to chat. A short conversation. A break. A bond.

"Papa, is this question from last year's paper?"

"Papa, mujhe aapke room ki whiteboard pe kuch explain karna hai."

Or simply, "Papa, chalna thodi der bahar?"

We often took those walks—outside the institute building, under the shade of old trees. Sometimes we discussed Physics, sometimes life. Sometimes we just walked.

He had a small habit—every other day, he'd stop at the Verka khokha just outside the institute and buy a packet of biscuits or a chocolate bar.

"Tumhe to bas bahana chahiye bahar jaane ka," I teased him once.

He smiled, munching on a biscuit. "Aur aapko bas koi topic chahiye samjhane ka."

We both laughed. In those small exchanges, a silent rhythm had developed. Not just of routine, but of a growing companionship. Of a student and a teacher. Of a son and his father.

And in those shared rides, quiet rooms, and biscuit breaks—his journey was slowly beginning to take shape.

CHAPTER SIX

Kul Devi and Conversations of the Soul

"Dadaji, subah massage ka time kya rakhna hai?" Yojan asked one Saturday evening while finishing dinner.

"Beta, 6 baje theek rahega? Main bula lunga," replied his grandfather with a gentle smile.

"Bas ek baar 'Yojan' keh dena, main aa jaunga," he responded with a grin.

And true to his word, no matter how late he slept—even 2 AM—at the simple call of "Yojan" from his grandfather, he would be up, ready with oil in hand. That one hour of massage every Sunday morning wasn't just about tradition. It was about connection.

As his hands moved gently over his grandfather's back, their conversation flowed with ease—studies, friends, worries, dreams. In that quiet space, they became more than just grandson and grandfather. They became friends.

"Dadaji, kabhi kabhi lagta hai sab mushkil hai," he confessed one morning.

"Hamesha mushkil rahega, beta. Par tum to mere fighter ho," his grandfather replied, smiling as he patted his hand.

Evenings carried their own sacred rhythm. Around 10 PM, his grandfather would quietly walk to Yojan's room.

"Beta, aarti ka time ho gaya."

"Bas 10 minute, Dadaji," came the usual reply.

His grandfather would sit patiently in the room, waiting without complaint. Within minutes, Bhawna or I would step in.

"Yojan, Dadaji wait kar rahe hain. Chalo."

And he'd spring up, as if on cue.

They performed aarti together, every single evening, almost without fail. The week was divided with different aartis for each day.

"Aaj kaunsa din hai, Dadaji?"

"Somvaar. Aaj Shivji ki aarti."

Their voices rang out in unison, high and clear, pouring energy into every word. And at the very end, Yojan would proclaim with booming enthusiasm—

"*Devi Chaimati ki Jai!*"

The whole neighborhood probably heard it. Bhawna and I would look at each other in that moment, smiling silently, a whole conversation exchanged without words.

The name had its own story. My mother, a tea lover, had earned the nickname "Devi Chaimati" from Yojan.

One day, our neighbor asked him, "Yeh Devi Chaimati kaun hai?"

He replied, with a straight face, "Hamari Kuldevi."

We all laughed for hours.

But beneath the jokes and rituals, there was something sacred in these bonds—daily rhythms that quietly shaped his strength, faith, and spirit. And without ever teaching, they taught.

CHAPTER SEVEN

Signs of a Journey

The start of Class 11 brought fresh energy. We began our daily commute again, Yojan and I. He'd carry that engineered cardboard box I had proudly made, using it like a table in the car.

"Papa, log ka base kaise change karte hain?" he asked one morning.

I glanced at him, thoughtful. Then without a word, pulled the car to the side.

"Dekho beta," I said, taking pen and paper from Yojan, "Base change ka simple rule yeh hai…" And there, by the roadside, began a mini-lecture.

This became a pattern—questions, quick stops, discussions.

But soon, signs of wear started showing.

His energy waned. I noticed a change in his posture. The boy who once sat upright with enthusiasm now sat with legs up on the table, books in his lap, shifting uncomfortably.

The plastic chair wasn't helping. One day, I saw him struggling—adjusting the chair, sliding forward, leaning back. That was it.

A new chair was purchased on top priority—a rolling one, with adjustable back and head support. His small study table on the bed remained, and a plastic washroom stool was placed beneath to relax his legs.

Soon, the table became a battlefield of books, notes, assignments, rough sheets. Only a tiny centre area remained clear for whatever he was currently working on.

After a quiet conversation with Bhawna, we replaced his table with a full dining table for more space. But the mess only grew—spreading, sprawling, like his thoughts.

One evening, as I stood at the doorway looking at that table—overflowing with dreams, pressure, chaos—I paused.

A thought stirred inside me. "Is this table the cost of chasing dreams?" I wondered. "Or the weight of a father's expectations?"

And somewhere in that quiet reflection, the idea of this book came back to me. To understand. To preserve. To share.

CHAPTER EIGHT

The Banner That Didn't Have His Name

Within a couple of weeks, the Class 10 result was out. Yojan scored 96%—a fantastic score, the best in our family so far. But he wasn't happy.

The reason wasn't the percentage. It was his position—4th in school. For the last 3–4 years, he had consistently been the school topper across all sections. This result felt like a setback to him.

But perhaps even the rank wasn't the real issue. The real pain came from a promise—one he had made silently to his Dadu: to get his photo on the school's topper banner.

The school printed only the top three students on its banner. And Yojan, being fourth, wasn't featured.

He didn't say much. But it was evident on his face.

He talked to his best friend Rohan—whom he lovingly called Mota. Rohan had chosen commerce and was continuing in the same school. He kept updating Yojan with all school news during those two years.

Rohan called to say, "Banner lag gaya hai school ke gate pe."

Though he was expressing concern that Yojan's name wasn't there, his words were like sharp pinches.

"Please Rohan, mat discuss kar," Yojan said once. But Rohan didn't stop.

That evening was heavy. His face had that silent gloom only parents can read. Bhawna and I sat together, watching him, exchanging glances filled with worry and quiet understanding.

We didn't push him to talk. Sometimes silence is a deeper conversation.

We also discussed the matter with my father. He gently tried to motivate Yojan, telling him it was perfectly fine not to be in the top three. He reminded Yojan that success isn't measured by banners, but by character, effort, and progress. But all went in vain. The conversation didn't seem to help him much.

He nodded along, but his eyes remained distant.

The banner stayed on his mind longer than we expected.

And in that quiet ache, the real challenge of this journey began—not of syllabus, but of spirit.

CHAPTER NINE

The One Who Set the Standards

It was an ordinary afternoon when something extraordinary happened—something that brought a quiet spark back into Yojan's eyes.

As he stepped out of the coaching centre, a voice called out behind him.

"Hello Bhaiya... Are you Yojan?"

He turned around. A younger boy, stood there nervously.

"Yes. What's the matter?" Yojan asked, curious.

"Nothing. I just wanted to see you," the boy replied shyly. "Even though you've passed school, your name is still there. Our SST teacher... she always gives your example in class. She still carries your notebooks. She says, 'This is how you write answers. This is how you maintain discipline.' I just wanted to see the guy who set such high standards."

Yojan didn't say much at the moment—just smiled slightly and thanked the junior. But as he sat in the car with me later that day, he couldn't hold it in.

"Papa, aaj kya hua suno..." he began, and narrated the entire incident with a quiet sense of pride glowing in his voice.

I listened without interrupting, letting him relive that moment of unexpected recognition.

Later that evening, as soon as we reached home, he rushed to the kitchen where Bhawna was preparing dinner.

"Mummy, ek baat suno..." he said, and repeated the entire story with the same excitement, this time with even more animated expressions.

She smiled, listening intently, placing a hand on his head by the end of it. "Beta, bas isi tarah achhe logon ki yaadon mein rehna," she said softly.

He nodded, eyes gleaming.

Actually, Yojan had always worked hard in school with one prime target—to impress his teachers and be in their good books. And he was totally successful in that. This recognition kept him internally motivated. Maybe the zeal of learning for the sake of learning would come later, but whatever drives a child to work hard in the right direction is perfectly okay.

Sometimes, the quiet admiration of a junior can remind you why you started. And sometimes, that's enough to keep going.

CHAPTER TEN

The First Setback

After three weeks of intensive study, it was time to test progress. A Sunday test was scheduled, and though the institute was officially closed for me, I still came along with Yojan .

The test went well—or at least that's what we thought.

The next day, Monday, while passing by the institute library, I caught a glimpse of Yojana through the glass door. He was sitting alone, deeply engrossed in reviewing his paper. I paused for a moment but decided not to disturb him.

Later that afternoon, the results were declared. The plan didn't sit well with us.

"Papa, my marks are less than what I actually scored," he said, trying to make sense of the mismatch.

I spoke to Mehak Ma'am, who was handling the test evaluation. She helped us recheck the responses. Every answer was carefully tallied with the scan records, and everything matched the declared result.

It was clear—the test hadn't gone as well as we had initially believed.

I was waiting in the car to drive him back home when he sat beside me, silent, lost in thought. I didn't ask much. His face said it all.

It was perhaps the first time he had truly tasted academic disappointment. For a boy who had consistently scored above 90% till Class 10, these marks felt like a crash landing. And this disappointment didn't pass in a day. It stayed, quietly building an invisible burden.

Something changed after that test. A quiet pressure seeped in—the fear of not being good enough, the anxiety of falling short. In class, Yojan became a little more hesitant. His hand no longer shot up first when teachers asked questions. A subtle sense of doubt started weaving into his once-confident self.

That Sunday test wasn't just about marks. It became a silent turning point—the beginning of learning how to deal with setbacks, with expectations, and with the battle within.

His schoolmate Gandhi, once his equal in school, was now being praised by teachers in class. Gandhi seemed to thrive in this new competitive environment. And unknowingly, I made the mistake of adding to the comparison.

"Gandhi is doing well," I had said one day. "Teachers were praising him in the staff room."

I meant to encourage, but perhaps all it did was pile on more pressure.

Looking back, I realize the comparison wasn't needed. I knew it, yet things happened naturally, unintentionally. Sometimes we, as parents, push without realizing where the edge begins.

And in that moment, I saw my son not just struggling with the syllabus—but wrestling with expectations.

His, mine, and the ones the world silently imposes.

Cracks Beneath the Numbers

Study and peer pressure were building up day by day. We could sense it clearly—on his face, in his eyes, in his silence. There was a fatigue that no sleep could seem to fix.

Trying to lift his spirits, I began adding little comforts to his routine. Fresh fruits, his favorite snacks, small surprises. Whenever lunch featured vegetables he disliked—kaddu, tinde, or lauki—I secretly ordered Lemon Cheese from Bansi through Zomato. The smile it brought to his face, even if momentary, made it all worth it.

Still, by the time we returned home in the evening, exhaustion would drape over him like a heavy cloak. To help him rest during our car rides, we ordered an eye blind—a black travel sleep cover.

At first, it helped. Some days he would get a decent nap. But most days, even with the eye blind on, I noticed him peeking through the edge, lifting it just a bit.

"Papa, mujhe thoda dekhna bhi hota hai... sirf soye rahenge to dimaag pak jaata hai," he said with a half-smile once.

He craved a break from the rigid rhythm of books and classrooms—needed to see people, traffic, movement. The world outside became his small escape.

Despite the exhaustion, the real concern emerged elsewhere. His performance, especially in Mathematics, began to slide.

That's when I decided to step in directly. I started preparing the chapters being taught in his class and tried to help him solve questions at home.

Every evening, we'd sit down at the study table.

"Beta, yeh question dekho," I'd say, picking one that looked simple to me. "Try karo, easy hai."

But the moment he began, stress shadowed him. His pen hesitated, his hand fumbled. Most of the time, he couldn't solve it in the first attempt.

"Papa, yeh mujhe samajh nahi aa raha," he'd say, eyes lowered.

"Samajh nahi aa raha? Arey dekho, yeh toh wahi pattern hai jo kal solve kiya tha," I'd point out, my voice raising a little without intending to.

"Main try kar raha hoon na!" he snapped one day, frustration breaking through.

I sighed, rubbing my forehead. "Yojan, tum try kar rahe ho par dekh nahi rahe. Questions ko feel karo... sirf solve mat karo."

"Papa, mujhe sab confuse ho raha hai. Har question alag lagta hai. Aap kehte ho pattern same hai par mujhe same hi nahi lagta," he said, voice trembling.

That evening ended on a bitter note. Again.

Each day we tried again. And each day, he struggled. He couldn't identify similarities, patterns, or connections between questions. And somewhere deep down, a fear began forming.

I now realize—perhaps my expectations were too high. I always *tried* to stay cool, but often, things went downhill.

Two unintended things happened.

One, I started lowering my expectations.

Two, a quiet but lasting fear of Mathematics found a home in Yojan's mind.

This is what I think today. Yojan's inner thoughts may be entirely different. But from where I stand, those evenings weren't just about Maths—they were about something bigger, something heavier.

And I wish I had seen it earlier.

CHAPTER TWELVE

The Strength Named Bhawna

Bhawna, his real hero—the only person who always stood firmly by his side.

She is a Chemistry Lecturer in a Government school. She never prepared for any competitive exams like JEE or NEET, neither as a student nor as a teacher. But that didn't stop her. She began preparing alongside Yojan, not for herself, but to support him.

Every evening, after wrapping up her schoolwork and household responsibilities, she would open Yojan's Chemistry books. She read chapters, made notes, searched doubts online, and listened to YouTube lectures—just so she could help him understand better.

This was no easy feat. Managing a full-time teaching job, the chaos of daily household chores, family duties, and on top of that, Yojan's JEE preparation—it was like walking a tightrope every single day.

Guests often visited in the evening—the exact time when Yojan and Bhawna sat down to study. Both would feel upset. Bhawna, torn between duties, would have one leg in the guest room or kitchen and the other in Yojan's study space.

This happened dozens of times over the two years. I witnessed it with my own eyes. Whenever I was home, I took care of the guests so Bhawna and Yojan could continue their study session uninterrupted.

But what amazed me most was Bhawna's ability to switch roles within seconds. At one moment, she would scold him:

"Yojan! Yeh question toh kal hi kiya tha, phir bhool gaye?"

And then the next moment, with the same enthusiasm, she would say,

"Chalo, main batati hoon phir se. Dekho, yahan pe mistake hui hai."

Her patience and determination were unmatched. I didn't have this talent. I tried, but many times I lost calm when things didn't go right.

One evening, while studying:

"Yeh question samajh nahi aa raha, Mumma," Yojan said, frustrated.

"Chalo, video dekhte hain dono milke," Bhawna replied. "Main pehle dekh leti hoon, phir tumhe samjhaungi."

Another time:

"Mumma, aapne yeh wala concept padha hai?"

"Abhi tak nahi. Par abhi padhti hoon. Tum dusra question karo tab tak."

Their teamwork was incredible. Silent. Consistent. Beautiful.

Just think—Yojan had the rare privilege of having two full-time teachers at home. I handled Physics. She handled Chemistry. We were available 24x7 for him.

Every night, I would go to bed around 10 PM. Often, Yojan would tiptoe into our room, holding his Physics notebook.

"Papa, ek sawaal puchhna hai," he'd whisper.

I'd blink awake from half-sleep, and answer—sometimes drowsily, sometimes with a full explanation.

He had full access to us—not just as parents, but as subject experts.

And in those moments, I couldn't help but think about the countless students out there—students who don't have this kind of support, who are struggling silently, alone in their battles.

It reminded me to be thankful, but also humble. Because privilege comes in many forms. And not everyone is lucky enough to have a Bhawna in their life.

CHAPTER THIRTEEN

Little Joys, Big Smiles

Despite the academic load, stress, and expectations, there were little pockets of joy that kept us all going—especially Yojan. These stress busters weren't scheduled; they just became part of our lives, naturally blending into our routine like silent healers.

One of our favorite activities was a simple game—pulling each other across an imaginary line in our lobby. Initially, I always won. My strength still had an edge. But slowly, as the months passed, I could feel the shift. By the end of Class 11, Yojan was comfortably dragging me over the line, his eyes sparkling with playful pride.

"Papa, ready?" he'd ask, gripping my hands with full energy.

"Aaj bhi main jeetunga," I'd grin.

He would laugh and say, "Bas dekhte jao!"

He started winning almost every game we played together. Carrom, table tennis, even random balancing contests. But there was one game where I still held my crown—hand wrestling. No matter how hard he tried, I never let him win that one.

"Yeh toh cheating hai," he would protest, laughing, "aap pura zor lagate ho!"

"Beta, kuch toh baap ka record rehne do," I'd tease.

Another thing that would break any tension instantly—tickling. Yojan had a secret weapon. He knew my weakness—my feet. Every time he wanted to make me laugh or change the mood, he would sneak up and start tickling.

"Yojan! Stop! STOP! Hahaha!"

"Bas ab mood theek ho gaya?" he'd giggle, enjoying every second.

And then there was his bathroom singing. A full concert, every morning. Sometimes it was Bollywood songs, sometimes bhajans, and occasionally, even Gita shlokas at full volume.

"Bhawna, suna tumne? Aaj Arijit Singh aur Krishna dono ek saath hain!" I'd joke.

She would smile warmly, "Dil se gaata hai, isiliye achha lagta hai."

We never stopped him. We just listened. Those few minutes filled the house with a kind of warmth that can't be explained—only felt.

Another constant companion of his was cricket. During matches, he'd keep one eye on the TV and one on his book.

"Papa, Kohli 82 pe hai," he'd whisper during a late-night session.

"Padho pehle, Kohli ka score badal jaayega, tera nahi," I'd reply with a mock stern look.

But updates kept coming.

His other favorite topic? Apple products. And he had a perfect partner for that—his Chachu, Dr. Sandeep Goyal, Assistant Professor at Allahabad University. The bond between them was not just of an uncle and nephew. It was friendship, camaraderie, and a shared world of curiosity.

"Chachu, iPhone 16 ki kya leaks aayi hain?" he'd ask over the phone.

Chachu would laugh, "Beta, tu toh Apple ka unofficial brand ambassador hai."

"Chachu, agar mujhe Apple ka CEO bana do na, main har saal 3 models nikaalunga," Yojan would joke.

"Pehle JEE clear kar, phir Tim Cook se baat karenge," Chachu would respond with a chuckle.

These small moments—games, tickles, songs, cricket chats, or tech talks—recharged him. Recharged all of us. They reminded us that no matter how hard the journey, the smiles along the way make it worthwhile.

CHAPTER FOURTEEN

Crisis Mode

Days turned into weeks, and weeks rolled into months. The syllabus kept expanding like a balloon about to burst. Alternate Sundays were reserved for tests, and they started coming in like a storm—frequent and ruthless.

There were murmurs in the institute—cheating during exams. It wasn't just a one-off. These complaints were echoing repeatedly, but no solid action was taken. And every such incident added to our anxiety. The whole point of testing was to gauge progress, and if that was compromised, what were we really doing?

I decided to take things into my own hands. To save time and ensure fairness, I began conducting Yojan's exams at home. Every Saturday evening, I would bring the question paper from the institute—like it was some top-secret government document. I didn't tell anyone. Not even Bhawna. I knew she would never misuse it, but the thrill of keeping it to myself pushed me to find new hiding spots each week. Under the mattress, inside an old file, wrapped in a towel—sometimes I even caught myself thinking, *"What the hell am I doing?"* But I still did it, religiously.

Sunday mornings turned into mini-JEE exams. Bhawna would mop the room, make sure the maid didn't barge in during the test hours, and prep the space like it was sacred ground. No one was allowed to speak loudly or walk in.

I would sit on the bed as an invigilator—watching over Yojan like a hawk, except with a laptop in hand and earphones plugged in, watching a movie. My eyes would dart to the screen and then back to Yojan. He sat on the chair, facing me, scribbling answers on the OMR sheet.

His answer sheets were submitted the next day to get them evaluated along with the rest of the batch.

But the results? They were still dipping.

No matter how hard he worked, how much we supported him, nothing seemed to reflect in the marks. The weight of it all was beginning to crush him. His eyes started losing their shine. He stopped smiling. The stress was visible—etched into his expressions, his movements, and the silence that lingered even when he was in the room.

One day, I saw he had bolted his room from the inside. We had never seen him do that. He wasn't the kind to shut himself away. We waited, anxious. The longer the door stayed closed, the higher our blood pressure climbed.

Bhawna finally knocked and told him firmly, *"Room lock nahi karna Yojan, samjhe? Kabhi bhi nahi. Agar kuch dikkat hai toh baat karo."*

But he didn't listen. The very next day, I quietly removed the bolt from his door. That one small action spoke volumes about our worry.

We were probably more stressed than Yojan himself.

One evening, the whole family was gathered in Mom and Dad's room for dinner. As always, Yojan finished his food first. He stood quietly near the door, his shoulders slumped. We could tell something was off.

I caught Bhawna's eyes. We both knew—it was the test result.

I took a breath and said something I never thought I'd have to.

"Yojan, don't worry too much," I said, my voice steady, trying to mask the tension underneath. "Even if JEE doesn't go well, I have enough money to get you into a good private college."

He looked at me, surprised. I pulled out his PPF passbook from the drawer and handed it to him.

"Dekho ismein... this is enough for the first year's fees at any top private engineering college in the state."

He didn't say anything. Just kept flipping through the pages.

Bhawna jumped in, "Aur beta, marks se zyada important hai ki tum apna best do. Jo ho raha hai, woh sab theek ho jayega."

Dadu, sitting at his usual spot, nodded slowly and added, *"JEE sab kuch nahi hai. Zindagi ka sirf ek chhota sa hissa hai. Mehnat jaari rakho, dil chhota mat karo."*

I chimed in, "You're doing great, honestly. Tum meri struggle wali story jaante ho. Tum toh usse kahin behtar kar rahe ho."

I went on to tell him about one of my old students—Aditya Chauhan.

"Bahut average student tha... lekin itna consistent tha na, ki aakhir NIT tak pahunch gaya."

That struck a chord. I could see a flicker of belief return to Yojan's eyes. The name "Aditya Chauhan" stayed with him. I knew that example etched itself somewhere deep in his mind.

Then, out of nowhere, he asked with a grin, "Agar main medical le leta... tab? 1 crore fees hoti private college ki... aap kara lete?"

I laughed, "Phir tum BDS kar rahe hote mere hero!"

Everyone burst out laughing. The heaviness in the air lifted, if only for a moment. And that moment was gold.

CHAPTER FIFTEEN

The Crossroads of Confidence

Till now, Yojan had been attending all JEE Advanced classes. It was part of the routine, part of the plan, part of the dream. But I could see what was really happening behind the scenes. His performance in regular tests was dipping, and when it came to the Advanced sessions, the feedback—what little I got—wasn't very encouraging.

I remember asking him one evening as we were driving back home, the sun casting long shadows on the road.

"Yojan, how was the Advanced class today?"

He looked out of the window and replied in a flat tone, "Theek tha…"

I glanced at him, "Koi question solve hua class mein?"

He hesitated for a moment, "Nahi… sab questions tough the. Sabse pehle Saanvi ne uthake kar diye."

"Tumne try kiya?" I asked, gently.

"Try toh karta hoon, but samajh nahi aata," he said, still avoiding eye contact.

This wasn't a one-time conversation. I had asked him many times over those weeks—same question, same tone in his replies. I could sense his growing detachment, the quiet acceptance of not being able to match the pace of those classes.

As a teacher, I knew what needed to be done. Continuing in those sessions would only burden him more, sowing seeds of inferiority and frustration. But as a father, it was harder—telling your son to step back, to let go of a path that was once filled with so much hope.

Still, I decided to act. I spoke to Rahul Sir, his Mathematics teacher.

"Sir, I think there's no point in him attending the Advanced sessions now. He's not ready. It's affecting his confidence."

Rahul Sir nodded in agreement. "I also feel the same. He looks lost in class. Better to focus on strengthening his base now."

I also discussed the matter with Ashwani Sir, his Physics teacher, who shared a similar sentiment.

And then, one evening at home, I broke the news to Yojan.

"Beta, ab se tumhe JEE Advanced ki classes attend nahi karni."

He looked at me. No shock, no resistance. Just a quiet nod.

"Samajh gaye?" I asked.

He simply said, "Haan, Papa."

We never spoke about it again.

Even though I knew this was the right call—one that would reduce pressure and help him refocus—my heart still worried. *Would he feel like he had failed? Would he start believing he's not good enough for JEE?*

But he never argued, never asked me to reconsider. Perhaps he understood, perhaps he was relieved. Or perhaps he was silently hurting and never showed it.

I wish I had asked.

But sometimes, silence is not a sign of agreement—just a way of coping. And still, as I look back, I believe he accepted the decision not just with maturity, but with a hidden strength that I had yet to fully understand.

CHAPTER SIXTEEN

Trophies and Truths

One afternoon, while searching for a book in Yojan's almirah, I accidentally knocked over a stack of his old trophies. As they clattered onto the shelf below, I paused and looked at them—golden, silver, and bronze reminders of a time that once made him shine.

There were awards from school dance competitions, science fairs, drama events, essay writing contests, Olympiads, and, of course, academic excellence certificates. Each one had a story, a memory, a spark. For Yojan, school life was nothing less than a golden era.

In school, he was a hero. Not just among peers, but even teachers who didn't teach him knew him by name. The school principal—Sister herself—would greet him with a smile. That kind of recognition, that warmth of being noticed and appreciated, it kept him going. It gave him purpose.

These trophies weren't just made of metal and wood. They were his fuel, his proof, his pride.

But now, life had changed.

That sparkle of confidence had dulled a little. He was no longer "the" Yojan—he was just "a" student in a classroom full of equally bright minds. The environment had shifted from applause to pressure, from appreciation to silent competition.

And I couldn't help but think—*how did we reach here so fast?*

A big part of the answer lies in the education system itself. CBSE has been reducing syllabus at the school level year after year, making the academic journey up to Class 10 appear smooth and manageable. But the moment a child steps into Class 11 with dreams like JEE or NEET, the whole world turns upside down.

The level of JEE has only been rising, year after year. Out of nearly 16 lakh students who appear, only the top 20,000 make it to the colleges of their choice. It's like being pushed off a cliff and expected to fly with no training.

After 14 years of CBSE schooling—starting from kindergarten—students are suddenly thrown into a new ocean in Class 11, expected to swim with sharks. No transition. No breathing space.

And most, including Yojan, are not prepared for that.

It's not about intelligence. It's about the shift. The gap between Class 10 and JEE level is enormous. And while many try to adjust, not everyone can cope.

Looking at those trophies, I realized something important: our education system does a great job of celebrating students till Class 10. But beyond that, it abandons them at the doorstep of unrealistic expectations.

I gently rearranged the trophies and closed the almirah door. They were shining still. And maybe, they were waiting for the day Yojan would shine again—with new dreams, new goals, and new victories.

Footsteps and Feelings

Evening walks became our little tradition. After dinner, the three of us—Yojan, Bhawna, and I—would step out into the quiet streets of our neighborhood. The purpose was never fitness. It was about those few minutes when we could just breathe, talk, and be together—beyond books, beyond results, beyond expectations.

These walks were our therapy sessions under the stars.

I would often start the conversation, "Toh Yojan, aaj kya padha? Kaisa laga?"

Bhawna would follow, "Koi naya trick ya concept samajh aaya? Batao na hum bhi seekhein."

Sometimes he answered with genuine interest, sometimes with a tired nod. But we kept asking, kept listening.

The walk continued, and as bikes zoomed past, Yojan's curiosity sparked. "Papa, yeh wali bike Super Meteor hai... Jagraon mein abhi tak sirf do hi aaye hain. This is the second one."

Then pointing at a house with soft yellow lights glowing inside, "Is house mein 4 cars hain—Audi, Creta, Fortuner, aur ek Safari. Bahar toh dikh hi jaati hain sab."

He'd chuckle as we passed the next gate, "Iss wali aunty bahut strict hain. Cricket ball andar chali jaye toh wapas nahi aati. Ek baar toh main chaar baar gate pe gaya... phir bhi nahi mili."

We'd all laugh, and Bhawna would suddenly disappear—her signature move.

"Arey Bhawna kahan gayi?" I would ask, looking around.

Yojan shook his head, "Mumma ki ye purani habit hai... ekdum se piche reh jaati hain bina bataye."

Then we'd see her walking slowly, grinning. "Aise hi mazaak karne ka mann kiya."

These moments gave us joy, a break from pressure.

But not every walk was all laughs.

One evening, Yojan's voice dropped a little as he shared, "Papa, ek teacher class mein kehte hain—'*Main sirf toppers ke liye padhaata hoon, baaki jo samajh paaye woh theek hai.*'"

I looked at him, quiet for a second. "Aur jab woh aisa bolte hain, kya feel hota hai?"

He shrugged, trying to hide the sting. "Feel hota hai... main class mein bas ek seat hoon. Face expression dekhta hi nahi koi. Agar unke favourite 4 students concept samajh lete hain, toh agli topic pe move kar jaate hain."

Bhawna immediately responded, "Beta, jo teacher sab bachchon ko equal importance nahi dete, woh khud apni teaching ka potential waste kar rahe hain. Tum toh apna best karte raho."

I added, "Classroom sirf toppers ke liye nahi hota. Har student apne tareeke se seekhta hai. Don't let those comments define you."

As we turned the last bend of our lane, I shared a thought that had been bothering me for days. "Kya pata beta... meri company kab tak chale. Kabhi kabhi lagta hai agar kuch unstable hua toh..."

Before I could finish, Yojan stopped me, "Papa, don't worry. Jab main job karne lagunga na, aapko kuch karne ki zaroorat nahi padegi."

That one sentence silenced both of us. Bhawna looked at me, eyes moist with pride. I just nodded, pretending I didn't hear the lump in my own throat.

Of course, we didn't want to stop working. We loved our professions. But hearing our child think of our comfort—*that* was the real reward.

These walks didn't solve problems. But they stitched us together—step by step, word by word.

CHAPTER EIGHTEEN

Health vs. Hope

It was a usual day between two classes when my phone buzzed. It was Rahul Sir.

"Chandan Sir, aaj Yojan class mein nahin dikha."

"Haanji sir," I replied, "He is not well... suffering from cold and cough. Kal class mein AC ka temperature bahut low tha. He's sensitive to such conditions."

I ended the call and leaned back, mind drifting toward home. Bhawna had taken off from school to take care of Yojan.

A few minutes later, she called, "Ji, which doctor should we consult? Dr. Garg for allopathy? Or Dr. Goyal for homeopathy? Ya phir Dr. Kamal Gupta? He's ENT specialist too."

I thought for a moment. "Garg's medicine will recover him quickly but will leave him tired. Goyal's homeopathy will take time... aur utne din classes miss ho jaayengi. Let's go with Dr. Kamal Gupta."

"Okay," Bhawna agreed, "I'll take him."

I paused before hanging up. "Aur suno... this isn't the first time. He *knows* the AC bothers him. I've told him so many times—keep a jacket in the car, use it when needed. But he doesn't listen. Tum samjhao usse. Maybe he'll listen to you."

She sighed. "Hmm, I will. But you also know how stubborn he is."

At home, the situation was different from what the institute could see. His immunity had started falling. His sleep schedule was completely off—sometimes dozing off at 2 AM, sometimes pushing himself awake till the early morning tests. That wasn't sustainable for anyone, let alone a teenager.

His snacking had taken over his meal routine. In between study breaks, he munched on his favorites—Biscoff and atta biscuits. There were wrappers lying around sometimes in his study drawer, sometimes in the car's backseat.

I often said, "Beta, do biscuit se kuch nahi hoga... par roz 10 biscuit se *bohot kuch* ho jaata hai."

But he would just smile and say, "Papa, ek break to banta hai."

Sports were long gone. The boy who was the fittest and slimmest in his class till 10th now carried about 20 kg more. That change wasn't just visible—it was alarming. His sharp jawline started softening, his posture lost its bounce, and most of all—his energy, the spark in his eyes, had dimmed.

I knew what was happening.

Health was being compromised—willingly, quietly—in exchange for a hopeful future, in the name of one dream: *one seat* in a good engineering college.

As a father, I was proud of his dedication.

As a teacher, I was worried about his balance.

And as a human... I just wanted him to sleep well, eat healthy, laugh more, and not forget that this journey, however competitive, is still a part of life—not life itself.

CHAPTER NINETEEN

IBBI Time – Struggles Beyond the Classroom

While Yojan was silently battling equations and expectations, I was juggling my own share of instability. My job had become like walking on a tightrope. A constant fear of the institute shutting down kept circling my mind.

I had already suffered—a 40% salary cut during the lockdown, three months without pay during a company transition, and then again, half-a-month's salary chopped off. I had mentally set a boundary: *no matter what, I will not leave my hometown.* This self-imposed constraint narrowed down my options drastically.

In that time of doubt and pressure, a ray of opportunity came through my cousin. He told me about something called *Certified Valuer*—a field I had never even considered before. I did my research and found I met the eligibility criteria.

Without wasting time, I registered for the mandatory training—four straight weekends, 9 AM to 6 PM. Those four weeks changed my schedule completely. Every evening after the classes, I would dive into notes, revise the new concepts, and try to grasp the unfamiliar terrain of valuation.

During this time, I was practically disconnected from the family. I couldn't help Yojan in studies, didn't even get time for small family talks. At home, I became a stranger sitting in one corner of the house with books and files.

But the challenge wasn't over yet. To become a certified valuer, I had to clear an exam.

I prepared... and failed. Missed the mark by 3.

It didn't have a direct impact on my current role, but emotionally, it hit hard. And I felt it even more when I thought of Yojan. *How could I motivate him to fight failure if I couldn't face mine?*

I gathered myself again. January and February were relatively free. I had some session-end leaves. I used this time to study with full focus.

But just one week before the exam, I got a call from Tejpreet Sir, my senior.

"Chandan, you need to be in HO, Bangalore. Urgent requirement."

I looked at the sky and said to myself, *Zindagi kab kis mod pe le aaye, pata hi nahi chalta.*

I failed again.

But I was clear—I might fail in the exam, but not in heart.

I couldn't afford to stop. I needed to show Yojan that giving up is not an option. I appeared once more, and this time... *I cleared it.*

Job was more stable now, and a backup plan was in hand. But the journey taught me something very important.

Struggles are not exclusive to students. Everyone is fighting a battle—some visible, some hidden. The stress of securing a seat in a good college is intense, yes, but it's a reflection of life's larger pattern.

Just like students carry the burden of expectations—personal, familial, and societal—so do adults. The only difference is that our timelines and targets differ.

Yojan was no exception. And now, neither was I.

CHAPTER TWENTY

Joy in Small Packets

Amid the pressure of weekly tests, continuous classes, and growing expectations, Bhawna found a beautiful way to ease Yojan's burden—*shopping in doses.*

Every Sunday, after his test, instead of letting the day end on a tiring or anxious note, we would plan a small outing. If Yojan needed five new pieces of clothing, we'd buy just one or two. This stretched the happiness across weeks instead of one big burst.

It was a clever trick. The kind only a mother could think of.

Every time Yojan got something new—a t-shirt, a hoodie, or even socks—his eyes would light up. The next morning, as he tried it on for the first time, he would quietly admire himself in the mirror. Not in vanity, but with a subtle, innocent pride. That look, just a few seconds long, where he would smile at his reflection—it was enough to fill our hearts for days.

We weren't lavish shoppers. Everything we bought was within our budget, nothing too fancy, and never in excess. Middle-class families don't run after brands; we run after moments. And this method of Bhawna's—of spreading out joy over multiple weekends—gave us more happiness than one big shopping haul could ever give.

We also got him sunglasses and shoes—one at a time, always giving something to look forward to. These weren't just purchases; they were quiet celebrations after the chaos of competition.

Another spark of joy came from a small voice on a screen—Tidda.

Sidhansh, lovingly known as *Tidda* because of his smaller height compared to his classmates, is Dr. Sandeep's son and Yojan's cousin. Their bond was something special—pure, unfiltered, and full of laughter.

Whenever Tidda called, our house transformed. His voice, bubbling with energy, filled not just Yojan's room, but every corner of our home.

"Bhaiyaaa! Dekho maine kya banaya!"
He would hold up a new drawing—sometimes an animal, sometimes a superhero.

Then he'd switch the camera, "Yeh dekho, naye shoes! Aur yeh sunglasses!" He'd give us a full tour of his latest acquisitions.

He even showed us yoga poses he learned in school, struggling but smiling through them. And Yojan, usually tired and quiet after tests, would burst into laughter, teasing him lovingly.

Sometimes, Yojan would take the phone and roam around the house, showing him what's new at our end. Tidda would inspect every corner—like a little home minister on duty.

The beauty of those calls was that they brought in a kind of warmth no shopping mall or relaxation technique could. It was love, bottled into a phone screen.

No matter how rough the week had been, one call from Tidda had the power to reset everything. And it wasn't just Yojan; even Bhawna and I would sit nearby, smiling silently, soaking in the affection of those moments.

These little things—shopping in pieces and calls from a tiny cousin—were our unexpected saviors. In a storm of syllabus and self-doubt, they were like gentle rain, reminding us that life isn't just about tests and targets.

It's also about *T-shirts and Tidda.*

Inertia of Motion, Instincts & Intensive Planning

It was the evening of January 20th. The air was crisp, the kind that lightly stings your cheeks but feels good after a long day.

We were returning home and had just passed the Grand Walk Mall when suddenly, from a narrow side street, a young boy on a bike came zooming in, without even slowing down. It was as if he had no clue what a brake was.

We were at a right angle to him.

"Papa, dekho!" Yojan shouted in alarm.

But I had already spotted him. My foot pressed hard—maximum pressure on the brake pedal. The car screeched and came to a halt barely a few centimeters before hitting the biker.

For a split second, everything went silent—except for a small crashing thud from the back seat. My laptop bag, tiffin bag, and Yojan's backpack had all toppled over.

Still stunned, I looked out the window, and with a mix of frustration and relief, I raised my right hand, circled my index finger at my temple, silently asking the biker—"Are you mad?"

The biker, clueless or embarrassed, sped away.

But before he completely disappeared, *both* of us shouted at the same time—

"Inertia of motion!"

We looked at each other, stunned, and then burst out laughing.

Only in a family of teachers and a JEE aspirant could a *near-accident* become a *live physics demo.*

That evening, something else happened too.

As we reached home and parked the car, I turned to Yojan.

"Yojan, 11th syllabus is over. Did you see the test planner on the group?"

"Haanji Papa, I saw it. But it's mostly JEE Advanced focused. We're not preparing for that level, right?"

"Yes, beta. I know. They're focusing only on top students now." I paused for a second and added,

"But don't worry. We'll make *our* plan. JEE Mains is our target—and we'll own it."

Yojan nodded, this time with a quiet sense of responsibility.

That same evening, Yojan and Bhawna sat down with pen and paper. Dates were written, chapters divided, weak topics highlighted. Each day was given a clear target—nothing too fancy, just focused and real.

Physics, Chemistry, Maths. Theory revision. PYQs. Backlog chapters.

Within an hour, the day-wise study planner was ready and pasted on the back of Yojan's room door.

"*Yeh kya hai? Timetable hai ya wall calendar?*" I teased.

Yojan smiled, "*Iss baar time waste nahi karna papa. Ek bhi din nahi.*"

From the very next day, the "Operation: 11th Revision" began. We worked as a team of three.

We formed a rotation rule:

- Day 1: I'd help with Physics,
- Day 2: I'd switch to Maths—I even studied a few tough topics myself to guide him better.
- Day 3: Bhawna would take over Chemistry—her energy never dipped, no matter how tired she was from school.

This rotation continued, week after week.

One evening, as we sat down for coffee after dinner, Bhawna chuckled,

"Yojan, do you know you're the only student in India with two full-time home tutors who also cook and clean?"

Yojan grinned, "You should start charging me. At least I'll learn to value this coaching properly."

We laughed. But deep down, we all knew this phase was special.

That revision period changed a lot. His confidence grew. He began solving problems faster, and—most importantly—believing in himself again.

One night, while solving a complex problem, he said,

"Papa, earlier this question looked like Greek. Now it feels like... maybe basic Sanskrit."

We both laughed, and I replied,

"Beta, Sanskrit bhi samajh aa jaayega. Just keep going."

More than the syllabus, more than the tests—it was this mindset that mattered.

That *nothing beats hard work*.

And hard work till the last day, as Yojan learned, was the

only real mantra for success.

And he did exactly that—till the last day of the second attempt.

But not every moment was serious and intense. Our study room had its own share of funny moments too.

One evening, just before starting a Physics revision session, Yojan was frantically flipping through shelves and drawers.

"Papa, PYQ ki book nahi mil rahi!"

"Aise kaise gayi? Abhi toh yahi thi," I replied while half-bent, checking under the table, behind the cushion, and even in the dustbin—don't ask why.

After a good 5 minutes of chaos and wild goose chase, Yojan finally gave up and shouted, *"Mummmmaa!! Dekhdo na please, yeh log toh kuch dekh hi nahi paa rahe!"*

Bhawna entered with her signature calm smile, walked straight to the pile next to Yojan's chair, lifted the top notebook—and there it was.

She handed him the book with that smug, unbeatable expression only moms have and said,

"Tum dono ko toh aankhon ke saamne bhi kuch nahi dikhta. Total andhe ho."

Yojan and I looked at each other, embarrassed and amused.

And then I broke into my specially composed jingle,

"Bhawna... Meri Pyaari Bhawna... Moti Moti Bhawna... Kya nahin bas tere...!"

All three of us burst into laughter.

Stress melted. The books opened again. And the journey continued—with a smile.

CHAPTER TWENTY-TWO

New Year, Same Grit

12th started—not with a bang, but with familiarity. Same alarm tone, same bus stop, same bag, and same morning hug from Bhawna before stepping out.

Routine had become a rhythm:

Home → Institute → Back Home → Dinner → Study → Sleep → Repeat.

Fortnightly tests came like clockwork—no surprise, no escape.

But one thing changed.

"Papa, mujhe classes ke baad wahaan rukna thoda zyada tiring lagta hai. I want to come home directly after lectures," Yojan said one evening while quietly folding his test papers.

I looked at him. He wasn't making excuses. He was exhausted.

"Thik hai beta. Come home after class," I replied, tapping his shoulder gently.

For the next few days, I used to drop him to the bus stop personally. It became our new ritual. A few quick words, a little advice, and a reassuring nod before he boarded the bus.

But routines never stay fixed for long. Within a few days, I was assigned doubt classes—right at the same time

Yojan needed to leave.

"*Papa, tension na lo. I'll manage,*" he said calmly.

Now, his return journey became a new adventure: sometimes a car cab, sometimes a bike cab, and many times, a classmate would drop him to the bus stop.

Travelling by bus was a completely new experience for him. A whole new world.

He started observing small things:

– The different ways bus conductors talk,

– How to negotiate for student fares or daily discounts,

– Who occupies the corner seats the fastest,

– The silent rules among co-passengers.

Every day he'd come back with a new tale.

"*Papa, ek conductor hai... har baar 5 rupees extra maangta hai. But aaj main nahi diya. Dikh gaya mujhe purana ticket...*" he said with a smirk.

Sometimes funny, sometimes frustrating, but all of it made him more aware, more street-smart. These rides became mini life lessons—less from books, more from the real world.

Days became weeks. Weeks turned into months.

Tests came and went.

Some were good, some average, some disappointing.

But one thing never changed—his consistency.

He didn't let poor marks pull him down, and didn't fly too high with good ones.

By the end of October, the 12th syllabus was completed in the institute.

And the revision of 11th started—round two of the race.

CHAPTER TWENTY-THREE

Rohan Saab – Dosti Wala Timeout

If there was one person who could shake Yojan's tightly packed JEE routine like a storm in a tea cup, it was *Rohan Saab* — his best friend, and probably the best teaser he'll ever have.

Rohan had a unique style of ensuring his presence was felt. If Yojan didn't answer his call, Rohan wouldn't stop there. He'd ring me next.

"Uncle, Yojan ka phone silent hai ya *JEE ke pressure mein* phone uthana bhi bhool gaya?" he'd say with a mock-serious tone.

Then Bhawna's phone would ring. Then Mom's. Then Dad's.

His logic was simple — "Agar Yojan ne call nahi uthaya, toh ghar ka har member uthayega."

And once Yojan finally called back, the floodgates of gossip opened.

"Bro, tere class ka Aditya fail ho gaya maths mein! Aur pata hai? Vandana ma'am ki scooter gir gayi — koi chot nahi lagi but pura school dekh raha tha."

He'd narrate each event like a cricket commentator — full of drama and unnecessary details.

And if school updates fell short, he'd switch gears.

"Shaadi aa rahi hai bhai... meri chachi ki beti ki. Dekh yeh suit photo, bata kaunsi shirt match karegi?"
"Dekh meri bullet! Nayi wali! Licence nahi hai, par style full hai."
"Police ne pakad liya, par chhod diya jab bola tuition ja raha hoon," he'd add with laughter that even made Bhawna giggle from the kitchen.

Yojan's reaction?

He'd argue, get irritated, hang up.

"Bas kar yaar Rohan! Mat kar call, padhai chal rahi hai!"

But within five minutes, his phone would ring again. Same caller. Same madness. Same friendship.

They'd argue, tease, laugh, and repeat the cycle like clockwork.

This was the kind of *fun* and *madness* that had been compromised during those intense two years of JEE preparation. Yet somehow, Rohan made sure a slice of it always found its way back into Yojan's life.

As parents, we used to overhear these conversations and smile quietly.

Because even in the pressure cooker of dreams and expectations, *a friend like Rohan was the valve that released just enough steam to keep the engine running.*

May this bond, full of love, madness, and relentless calls, stay forever.

CHAPTER TWENTY-FOUR

The Form, The Test, and The Silence

It was that time — the final step before the real beginning. Filling the JEE form.

I opened the portal with the seriousness of a surgeon ready for operation.

Each field — Name, Father's Name, School Name, Category, ID Number — I typed, paused, checked, and re-checked. Every letter mattered. Every digit was double-checked. My eyes scanned the screen like a radar, ensuring nothing went unnoticed.

Just before submitting, I called Bhawna.

"Ek baar aur check kar le na... naam, date of birth sab kuch."

She laughed, "Itni baar dekh chuke ho, ab toh form bhi bol raha hoga bas karo!"

Then I called Yojan.

"Beta, last check tu kar le — name, school, paper code, sab kuch sahi hai na?"

He glanced through and chuckled, "Papa, itna dar kyun lag raha hai? Aap toh engineer ho... teacher bhi ho... itna formal fear?"

They both started teasing me. But I was too deep in the moment to care.

For them, it was a form.

For me, it was the entry pass to the dreams we had nurtured for years.

A few days later was Yojan's first revision part test.

Me and Bhawna had to attend a *bhog* at Patiala. It was a family obligation, but our minds were still half-occupied with the exam.

At around 1 PM, my phone rang.

Yojan.

I answered quickly, expecting an update like always.

"Papa... main blank ho gaya paper mein. Kuch samajh nahi aaya. Paper chhod ke bahar aa gaya hoon..."

His voice was low. Almost trembling. My heart sank.

I wasn't angry.

I wasn't disappointed.

I was just quiet.

Something inside me whispered — not now. Don't question. Don't react. Just listen.

I replied calmly, "Koi baat nahi beta. Jo ho gaya, so ho gaya. Ab agli test ki tayari karo. Main tum par vishwas karta hoon."

That was all I said. Because I knew, he had already said the hardest thing.

Later that day, *Neeraj*, his mammu, came to know. He called Yojan instantly.

"Yeh kya kiya tune? Part test ka paper blank chhod diya? Pressure mein kaise har maan sakta hai?"

It wasn't a scolding — it was concern, in the tough tone of a loving uncle.

Maybe Yojan wasn't ready for the finals just yet. Maybe pressure took over preparation. Or maybe he needed to fail that day to stand stronger the next.

But one thing was sure — we didn't treat this moment as a failure.

We treated it as a part of the journey.

Because like Bhawna always says, "Har bada sapna, kabhi na kabhi to darrata hi hai."

And that day, the silence of a skipped test spoke louder than a hundred attempts.

CHAPTER TWENTY-FIVE

28th January – First Attempt

Life had entered a loop — eat, study, revise, test — repeat.

After that first stumble, we were back at it again. The plan was rebuilt, reshuffled, and repasted — on the back of Yojan's room door, just like before. This time it was tighter, more focused. We were targeting *PYQs* — Previous Year Questions — like a laser.

I took charge of Physics. Bhawna commanded Chemistry. Maths? That was Yojan's domain.

While revising with him, I started preparing short notes for every chapter — he could use for CBSE and second attempt later. No pressure. Just preparation. That was our mantra.

Pressure was in the air, thick and invisible, but we had made a silent pact —

"We won't judge him, no matter the result."

The exam date arrived: 28th January, morning shift.

But for me, the actual battlefield was 26th Jan.

That day, I became the General of Operation JEE:

- Printouts were taken — three copies, just in case.
- Photos pasted perfectly.

- Thumb impression checked — twice.
- Transparent water bottle? Yes
- Transparent pens? Yes
- Transparent file cover? Yes

NTA ka rule book yaad ho gaya tha mujhe.

28th morning, alarms rang at 5:00 AM.

Mom prepared breakfast to pack. Everything was kept ready like we were going on a pilgrimage.

We left by 5:40 AM, the center was 1.5 hours away, but fog had its own plans.

Better to be early than stressed on the road.

We reached safely.

Yojan ate his breakfast in the car, quiet but calm.

At 7:45 AM, he waved and entered the exam center.

Bhawna and I stood outside... waiting.

Surrounded by hundreds of parents, we exchanged stories, nervously laughed, spoke about everything except the thing sitting on all our hearts.

Because the truth was:

This exam was not just his. It was ours too.

The past two years — late-night doubts, skipped parties, missed vacations — had made it a shared journey.

12:00 noon.

Parents rushed to the gates, necks stretching to get the first glimpse of their children.

We managed to push forward, standing right in the front.

And then, we saw him.

Yojan, walking out... his face pale, his hand raised dramatically.

He moved it across his neck like a knife — the classic sign of "It's over."

Our hearts sank.

He came closer. No words.

Just a sigh. His eyes wet, not with tears, but with defeat.

We didn't ask a single question.

We handed him snacks. Let him eat.

The car ride back was mostly silent.

Just quiet hums of the road and the occasional word from Yojan about the paper.

"Papa, paper bohot tough tha... bahut logon ne attempt bhi kam kiya..."

We just nodded.

And told him gently, "It's okay beta. First attempt hi tha. Abhi ek aur chance hai. Aur hum sab tere saath hain."

CHAPTER TWENTY-SIX

When the Clouds Hovered Low

The answer key was out.

With slightly trembling fingers and a mind clouded with doubt, I sat down to calculate Yojan's probable score. Below 100. My heart sank. Though somewhere deep I had sensed it, confirming it through numbers stung even harder. I didn't share the score with anyone. Not even Bhawna. Not even Yojan. It was a quiet storm inside me.

A day later, while returning home, I received a call from Tejpreet Sir. "Result kaisa aaya?" "Uska kya result aana hai," I replied, half in jest, but more in resignation. I had already made peace with the fact that this attempt was not the one.

And then came the official JEE result. A 90 percentile. In other words, he was ahead of 90 percent of students. But in the brutal world of JEE rankings, that translated into a rank close to 1,60,000. No dream college. No NIT. Not even a strong private option.

There was silence in the home. Thick, heavy silence. Even my mother, who normally asked questions freely, asked about the result in a whisper. Everyone could read the disappointment in my face. My efforts to motivate Yojan were met with forced smiles. He was trying to be normal too, but the air was heavy, and we all felt it.

The next morning, I got a call from Dr. Sandeep—Yojan's chachu. When I told him the result, the silence from his side spoke volumes. He didn't shout, but his disappointment pierced me more than words ever could. I felt it deeply.

But there was no time to wallow.

The toppers at the institute were now focused on JEE Advanced. But for us, the next checkpoint was the CBSE Board exams. We knew exactly what needed to be done. Yojan had to give his best here—because a polished Class 12 performance would prepare him better for the second JEE attempt.

And with that came two new battlegrounds: Physical Education and English.

Subjects Yojan hadn't studied all year.

Bhawna, the real hero of our story, stepped up. Once again. She researched books, ordered a fresh set of NCERTs, PYQs, and question banks. She didn't stop there. She watched YouTube lectures, took down notes, explained meanings of tricky words, and even made fun mnemonics to help Yojan remember. Chemistry was her main battlefield, but she carried Physical Education and English like extra luggage with a smile.

How she did it, I still don't know. I don't think many could have. Hats off to her unwavering dedication.

We went into battle mode again. This time with better clarity. I took full charge of Physics three days before the exam, just like always. Bhawna ensured that other subjects were in line. Yojan, to his credit, managed Maths by himself like a seasoned warrior.

As the exam days approached, the tension was real, but so was the unity. We had a plan. We had our roles. And most importantly—we had each other.

Yojan's board exams went well, as per his feedback. But we weren't in a mood to assume anything. We had learned to keep expectations measured and hearts hopeful.

The results would tell their own story. But one thing was certain—this chapter wasn't about failure. It was about standing tall even when the clouds hovered low.

CHAPTER TWENTY-SEVEN

Ram Payari – Our Silent Companion

Our car, lovingly named **Ram Payari** , was more than just a vehicle during those two crucial years—it was our silent companion, our family member on countless journeys.

While Yojan remained buried in his studies during travel, solving problems, watching concept videos, or simply revising notes, I had another focus altogether. I was always busy calculating time and distance, almost like a personal project.

" Yojan , it took 24 minutes to reach Mullanpur today. We are two minutes late compared to yesterday!" I would announce proudly, as if declaring the stock market figures.

Without even looking up, Yojan would reply, half-smiling, "Papa, it's unwanted and irrelevant data. You are the only one maintaining these records!"

Sometimes, I would add, "Today's car average is showing 25 km/l. Yesterday it was 28 km/l. See the drop?"

He would chuckle and tease, "Papa, one day it will show 35 km/l, and you'll write a research paper on fake car mileage!"

Ram Payari wasn't just a machine; she was part of our family moments.

Whenever my friend Rupesh's Chacha ji and his family needed a lift to Jagraon or a return ride to Ludhiana, Ram Payari was ready. No questions asked.

I still remember one evening when Rupesh called me, "Bhai, please pick up Chacha Ji today evening, please."

I replied laughingly, "Remind me once in the evening. You know how forgetful I am!"

Rupesh chuckled, "Hey brother, I am worried about the reminder no Do it ! You will get not one but three or four calls . One from me , one from father and two from uncle . You are sure. Bhool no I can !"

And sure enough, that evening, the phone didn't stop buzzing—first Rupesh, then his father, and then two enthusiastic calls from Chacha ji himself!

Similarly, my cousin Rozi and her daughter often traveled with us. Rozi's daughter was actually Yojan's batchmate. Naturally, they always had plenty to chat about—mock tests, tough assignments, funny incidents in coaching classes. Their excited conversations filled the car and added another flavor to our otherwise quiet rides.

Sometimes, during these long drives, Yojan would talk with such maturity—sharing deep thoughts about life, studies, or even philosophy.

In those moments, I would jokingly say, "You are getting enlightened! I think it's because of your seat. This seat has some magic powers."

And without missing a beat, on other occasions when I said something wise, Yojan would laugh and say, "Papa, you are also getting enlightened! Looks like some radiations are being showered on you too!"

It became our little in-car joke—blaming all our newfound wisdom on the magic of Ram Payari's seats.

Sometimes, Ram Payari even acted like a courier service—handing over goods to Satnam's Massi ji or bringing something back for Satnam Singh. She carried not just passengers but pieces of life, stories, and goodwill.

Every small thing related to the car was recorded religiously—fuel expenses, tolls, servicing—all neatly logged into a notebook stored in the dashboard.

"Papa, you track Ram Payari's expenses better than my exam scores!" Yojana would joke.

And I would grin and say, "Beta, whether it's a car or a career, tracking small things helps you drive the bigger journey better."

Ram Payari was not just about rides. She was a vessel of our dreams, laughter, anxieties, and hopes—a humble witness to our two-year-long journey.

Sometimes, even today, when I drive alone, I find myself glancing at the passenger seat instinctively—as if expecting Yojan to be there, lost in his books or cracking a joke.

Whenever he is not with me, a certain emptiness rides along. I miss him deeply—his quiet presence, his curious questions, his little arguments. Ram Payari carries those memories too, silent but alive, whispering through every mile we travel alone.

Turmeric Milk, Mornings, and Dreams

"Yojan, get up! It's already 7," Bhawna's voice echoed through the room as she placed a mug of warm turmeric milk by his side and rushed back to the kitchen.

Still half-asleep, Yojan mumbled, "Dadu..."

Dadu was already waiting for this call. "Aaya," he replied with a soft chuckle.

A new family ritual had quietly formed—Yojan's daily head massage. Most mornings and even some evenings, someone in the house—usually Dadu—would gently rub his head or press his eyes. It wasn't just comfort; it was therapy. A small act of love against the massive weight he was carrying.

His stress had clearly taken a toll. Sleep hours had shrunk to five. Exercise was forgotten. Biscuits had become his constant companions. He had gained enough weight for family members to start calling him "Mota," though it was always said in jest, not judgment.

His immunity was down. Cold and cough became frequent visitors. One day, worried about his persistent headaches, I went to Dr. Garg. I even hesitantly asked if some mild stress-relieving medicine could be prescribed.

But Dr. Garg strictly refused. "Not at this age," he said. "No shortcuts. Let him rest more, eat well, and release the pressure."

We followed the prescription religiously, but nothing seemed to work magic.

One particular morning, as Dadu massaged Yojan's head, I overheard a candid conversation.

"Dadu, engineering is just a backup plan for me," Yojan said softly.

"In engineering college, I'll follow my real passion—dance. Or maybe, I'll start a business."

"Kya business karega?" Dadu asked curiously.

"Not decided yet," Yojan replied, half serious, half dreamy.

Dadu smiled, "In India, most people first do engineering and then decide what they want to do."

Then, after a thoughtful pause, he added, "No issue. One should always choose a profession that makes them happy. There's no point doing something if your heart's not in it. I am always with you."

Yojan's face lit up.

"Dadu, when I start earning, I'll buy an Enfield bike. I'll take mom and dad on a world tour. And I'll go with Mammu to watch a cricket match at Lord's!"

Dadu laughed, kissed his forehead, and said, "Bas, khush reh beta. Teri khushi mein hi sab kuch hai."

In that moment, amidst the stress, the turmeric milk, and the quiet conversations, something beautiful was brewing—hope.

And that was enough to begin another day.

CHAPTER TWENTY-NINE

The Calm Before the Second Storm

A couple of weeks were left for the second attempt. The pressure was still there—but this time, I decided to step back.

I stopped interfering much. Let him breathe. Let him find his own flow.

He came to me for about half an hour every day to ask Physics doubts. That was our time. Focused. Crisp. No lectures, just clarity.

Maths—as always—he handled himself. It was his toughest subject. I could see it, sense it. He even hesitated asking questions from Rahul Sir. I never forced him. Maybe he needed to wrestle with it himself.

Chemistry became a joint mission for Bhawna and Yojan. They sat together daily, solving, discussing, repeating. Bhawna had practically become an expert in the subject by now.

And then began the phase of online mock tests. He appeared for one after another. We never asked for his scores. Never. Only one thing mattered: "Clear your doubts from these tests." That's all we told him.

But unknown to him, I was getting his scores anyway.

My email ID was linked with the test series portal, and after every mock test, I would receive detailed analytics: score, percentile, accuracy, everything. I saw the graphs. I knew where he stood. But not once did I share those numbers with Bhawna or Yojan. This wasn't the time to critique. It was the time to protect his calm.

April 3rd.

I was in the staff room at work when my phone buzzed with multiple WhatsApp messages. All from Yojan. All filled with doubts. One after the other.

Rahul Sir was sitting beside me.

I turned the phone toward him and said, "Sir, I don't know what he'll do tomorrow or what his result will be. But the boy is fighting. He's asking questions, till the last moment. He's still trying. That's enough for me. I'm satisfied with this."

Rahul Sir nodded and smiled, "This is exactly what matters. This is what one can do."

We both smiled, silently praying.

That same evening, we followed the ritual.

His kit was ready—roll number printout, Aadhaar card, transparent pen pouch, water bottle, everything according to the NTA norms. His thumb impression on the admit card. Packed carefully in a transparent file cover. Placed on the front seat of the car.

The battleground was ready.

Tomorrow would be the second attempt. A new chance. A new sunrise.

But tonight, we just wanted peace.

CHAPTER THIRTY

The Second Attempt

April 4th.

The morning was quiet, but our hearts weren't.

We all woke up at 5:30 AM. The air felt heavier than usual. This wasn't just another exam day—it was *the* day. The second attempt. The redemption shot.

This time, the center was a little close —about 20 kilometers away in Mullanpur Dakha, coincidentally on the same route as my office. The plan was clear: Yojan and I would go together. Bhawna, after already taking nine leaves for his preparation, had to attend school today. Her heart wanted to come, but duty called.

Sweet curd was served, as per tradition. Prayers were whispered. Blessings were taken from both grandparents, each with folded hands and hopeful eyes. And then, just after 7 AM, we departed.

By 7:30, we reached the examination center. It was still early.

I found a shady spot to park the car. There was time to breathe, to calm the nerves. I pulled out a small bar of his favorite—**Oreo Silk**—and handed it to him like a charm. He smiled, took a bite, and opened his notebook for a last-minute scan. Revision, prayers, a little chocolate—everything had its place.

Around 8, we walked towards the gate. I stayed outside the entry point for another twenty minutes, just to ensure everything went smoothly—ID, admit card, biometric, entry. The plan was for him to return with his friend Krishna after the exam.

But my heart... it wasn't ready to leave.

I went to office, sat for my lecture, delivered it—but I wasn't present. I couldn't focus. His exam, his silence, his past, his future—it was all clouding my thoughts. I kept glancing at the clock, wondering what was happening in that examination hall.

After my lecture ended, I didn't think twice. I got up, sat in the car, and drove the 25 kilometers back to his center.

I waited outside. This time, I wanted to *see* him. *Feel* his mood. I didn't care how far the drive was. Every minute felt like an hour.

And then, finally, he walked out.

He wasn't expecting me.

That moment. That expression. Relief. Surprise. A little smile. A glimpse of hope.

We talked briefly.

"Physics went well."

"Chemistry was good, though I made a few guesses."

"Maths was tough. I attempted only four."

But despite the difficulty—he was *happy*. And that was enough for me.

He left with Krishna. I returned to my office, but my mind stayed with him.

Within two hours, we were both glued to YouTube. Shift reviews, expert analysis, paper discussions—everything. The general opinion: the paper was tough.

Yojan kept sending me links. I kept watching and cross-checking.

And then came the mind games—"*99 percentile tak kaise jaayega?*", "*Negative marking jyada toh nahi ho gayi?*"

I told him, "Beta, so ja. Sleep now."

But of course, there was no sleep. Not for him. Not for me.

Because when your heart is still in the exam hall, how can the body rest?

In the afternoon, Yojan came to me with a calm but determined look on his face.

"Papa," he said, "this attempt went well. I'll work even harder now. I'm sure my VIT exam will go better than JEE Mains, and BITSAT Attempt 1 will be better than this one. BITSAT 2 will be the best. I'm confident I'll get admission into a good college."

His words weren't just hopeful—they carried the weight of resolve, shaped by experience and effort.

CHAPTER THIRTY-ONE

The Calm After the Storm

It was time to relax.

Yojan woke up around 9 AM—no alarm, no hurry, no schedule. For the first time in what felt like forever, the morning began without a list of tasks or a looming exam. It was a full day of leisure.

He tried calling Rohan, his old partner-in-stress, but Rohan was already neck-deep in his new path, preparing for CA. So Yojan had the next two days entirely to himself—no books, just downtime. He went shopping with Dadi and Mom, enjoyed slow walks with Krishna, and let the calm soak in.

At home, Bhawna and I began clearing out his study corner. The shelves were overflowing with books—some read cover-to-cover, others barely touched. Yojan stood nearby, watching us sort through the stack.

"Yeh rakh lo na, ismein meri Chemistry ki notes hain," he said, holding up a crumpled notebook.

"Beta, notes rakhenge... par yeh twenty mock tests ki copies toh jaane do," Bhawna smiled.

"Bas trophies ko mat hila dena," Yojan quickly added, pointing to his carefully placed collection.

"Woh toh rahengi jahan hain. Reminder hai ki mehnat ki thi," I said.

Books that could still be of use were taken to my academy and distributed to students who needed them. The rough copies—those dog-eared, ink-smeared warriors—were sold to a scrap vendor for 300 rupees.

And just like that, the weight of two years found its way out the door.

The next family event was Yojan Bua's 'Mata ki Chowki'. For the first time in two years, we were going for a family function with no stress tagging along. No one carried books. No one was checking test papers in the back seat. The car was filled with music, laughter, and light-hearted banter.

Yojan even took the wheel and drove more than 100 kilometers. A milestone pending for far too long.

Another few days of this calm remained before VIT and BITSAT preparation would begin. But for now, peace had finally made its home in ours.

In the past week, he hadn't asked for a head massage. No painkillers. No stress spikes. Just silence—and a much-needed pause.

It wasn't the end of the journey. But it was a much-deserved breath.

And sometimes, that's all you need to feel alive again.

CHAPTER THIRTY-TWO

The Silence Before the Next Sunrise

For the last two days, Yojan had been at his Mammu's house. A well-deserved break.

They even went to watch an IPL match in Mohali—something he'd been longing for all year. The cheer of the crowd, the bright lights of the stadium, and the sound of leather meeting willow... it was his moment of escape. And he looked so happy in the photos Mammu sent.

Back home, though, things felt different.

The house was unusually quiet. His room, once a battleground of books, notes, and alarms, now felt too neat, too still. Bhawna was folding laundry in the living room when she suddenly said, "Pata hai, kal bina chillaye subah ho gayi..."

I smiled and replied, "Woh toh jaise ek aadat ban gayi thi na—'Yojan, uth ja!'..."

We both laughed, but the silence that followed said more than words ever could.

There was a strange emptiness in the air. We were missing him terribly. And along with that, came a lingering thought—what would it be like when he actually leaves for his college? When this silence becomes routine, and the coffee mugs are always clean because he's not around to leave one half-finished in the room?

But life, as they say, must go on.

The answer keys were expected in a day or two. Final ranks would follow within the week. Yet, none of us were overly anxious anymore. We were... prepared. For anything.

We had seen him rise, fall, break, rebuild, and still walk on with grace. That was enough for us.

"Chaahe jo bhi result aaye... usne jo kiya, dil se kiya," Bhawna said one night, holding a cup of tea, staring blankly at the ceiling.

"Bas yeh yaad rahe... Learning in any form never goes to waste," I replied. "Even if he didn't master PCM, he learned something far more important—how to stand when every wind blows against you."

Yojan had matured beyond his age in these two years. He had tasted defeat, disappointment, anxiety—and still managed to walk into his exam with courage, with a smile. That's no small feat.

I remember one evening, just before he left for Mammu's place, I asked him, "Kaise lag raha hai ab sab ke baad?"

He took a deep breath and said, "Baba, lagta hai ab thoda samajh aa raha hai life ka pace. Jab sab kuch ulta chal raha ho, tab rukne ka mann karta hai. Par agar ruk gaye, toh shayad wapas uthna mushkil ho jaata hai."

I just placed a hand on his shoulder. "Zindagi sabse pehle test leti hai, phir sikhati hai," I said.

He smiled.

There's still a long road ahead—VIT, BITSAT, final counselling, and a whole new chapter of college life. But for now, we are at peace.

The storm has passed. The skies may still be cloudy, but there's light on the horizon. And most importantly, the sailor is stronger than ever.

• 83 •

Growth Beyond Results

As we come to the end of this journey, it's important to reflect on the path we've walked together—through struggles, setbacks, and triumphs. The story of Yojan's JEE preparation is not just a chapter of academic rigor but also a testament to the resilience of the human spirit. It is a reminder that success is not always measured in terms of ranks or accolades but in the strength we develop while facing challenges.

This journey was never easy. There were moments when we doubted ourselves, when the pressure seemed too much to bear. Yet, in the face of adversity, we found our strength. We realized that it wasn't about being the best in the race but about learning how to stand tall when the path ahead seemed unclear.

To Yojan, my son—this is your story. You have shown tremendous courage and determination, and we are incredibly proud of you. Your effort, your commitment, and your resilience will carry you far beyond any exam or result. You have learned lessons far more valuable than any rank can offer. Your journey is just beginning, and the world is full of opportunities waiting for you to explore.

To Bhawna, my incredible partner—this book would not have been possible without you. Your unyielding support, love, and sacrifices have shaped this journey, and your dedication to both Yojan and the family is unparalleled. You are the true hero behind the scenes.

To all the JEE/NEET aspirants and their parents—this book is for you. The pressure, the stress, the long nights, and the uncertainty are all part of this journey. But remember, no effort goes wasted. The lessons learned in these moments will serve as the foundation for everything you build in the future.

Finally, to everyone who has walked this journey with us, supported us, and shared their experiences—thank you. Your encouragement, whether it was through a kind word or a simple gesture, helped us navigate through one of the most challenging yet rewarding times of our lives.

The journey may be over, but the story continues. And in the end, it's not about the results; it's about the growth, the lessons, and the memories we carry forward. Life has much more to teach, and we are ready for whatever comes next.

Lessons Beyond The Rank

1. As Parents – Behind Every Tense Equation, a Tender Emotion

The JEE journey tested our roles as parents in unexpected ways. We weren't solving problems on paper, but we were solving problems of the heart.

Emotional Support > Academic Pressure

There were days when Yojan sat blankly in front of his books. Pushing him harder didn't help. But sitting beside him, talking about life, or just playing a board game made a huge difference. We realized—sometimes the best way to help your child study is to help them smile.

Safe Spaces Matter More Than Study Spaces

We tried to keep the atmosphere at home light, especially during stressful days. A joke over dinner, a walk around the colony, or Bhawna's chai breaks brought calmness amidst chaos. Mental peace became as essential as mock tests.

Percentile Doesn't Define Potential

After the first attempt, it was hard to not feel disappointed. But slowly we taught ourselves to celebrate Yojan's resilience, not his rank. He didn't give up, and that was more valuable than any percentile.

Our Invisible Roles

From ironing his clothes on exam days, hiding his favourite snacks in drawers, or massaging his head at night—our contributions didn't reflect on a mark sheet. But we knew they mattered.

Balancing Involvement and Independence

We had to remind ourselves—Yojan isn't *us*. He needs to fail, learn, adapt. We stepped in when needed but also gave him space to take ownership.

2. As Teachers – Beyond Syllabus and Solutions

Being an educator who trains students for JEE/NEET gave this experience a dual lens.

Each Child Has Their Own Algorithm

I saw my own teaching philosophy evolve. Yojan wasn't the same as other toppers. He had his own pace, his own style. No formula fits all.

Empathy is the Real Education

I saw firsthand how even the most brilliant minds struggle emotionally. As teachers, our role is not just academic but human. A soft voice, a listening ear, or a well-timed joke goes a long way.

Mental Health is Not Optional

I had taught hundreds of students, but never paid enough attention to their inner battles. With Yojan, I realized anxiety can silently ruin performance. It changed how I approached students in class too.

Be a Guide, Not a Guard

Even though I was his father and a teacher, I avoided spoon-feeding him. Instead, I encouraged him to ask questions on his own terms.

Real Life Lessons Aren't in NCERT

We discussed failure, career paths, handling pressure, and finding joy in the journey. These became the moments where true teaching happened.

Never Say "We Are Only Concerned for Rankers"

This one line can destroy the confidence of many students. Every child deserves attention, regardless of rank. Teaching is not about securing results; it's about nurturing potential. I promised myself to never use this phrase.

3. As a Student – More Than Just PCM

Failure is Feedback, Not Final

Yojan's first attempt was a blow, but he used it to reset. He didn't crumble. He picked himself up. And in that, he matured more than in any Chemistry class.

Resilience is a Skill

He learned to bounce back, manage time, and prepare despite distractions. He adjusted when he needed to shift focus to boards. He found new methods and kept going.

Discipline Builds Dreams

There were no late-night movie marathons, no weekend outings. Every hour was planned. Even when motivation dipped, the habit kept him going.

Dreams Can Evolve

What started as an engineering dream gradually widened into bigger questions: "What do I love?" "Where do I want to go?" "What is success for me?"

Family is the Silent Backbone

He may not have said it aloud every day, but we saw it in his eyes—the gratitude, the comfort, the strength he drew from the home team.

4. When the Destination Shifts – Alternate Roads to Success

JEE Isn't the Only Door

Not cracking IIT or NIT is hard, but not the end. We realized success has many routes—some even better aligned with the student's personality and passion.

College Doesn't Define Career

We researched and found success stories from VIT, SRM, BITS, and even lesser-known colleges. It's what you make of it.

Options Beyond Engineering

Yojan explored interests in dance, business, and storytelling. We encouraged these thoughts. Today's world offers endless paths—from design and law to CA, content creation, and coding bootcamps.

Study Abroad is a Viable Option

With proper planning, scholarships, and research, students can find world-class education outside India too.

A Gap Year Can Be a Gold Mine

Taking time to reassess, strengthen weak areas, or even intern or travel can give students clarity before their next step.

Skills Matter More Than Colleges

Coding, communication, confidence—these open more doors than a brand name. We focused on building real-world abilities.

5. Lessons That Weren't in the Syllabus

We thought this journey was about JEE. But it was actually about:

- Understanding our child better
- Redefining our expectations
- Relearning how to support, not push
- Recognizing what really matters in the long run

JEE was a test on paper. But life's real test was how we stood together, adapted, and grew.

And in that—we passed with flying colours.

No matter what the result may be, our strength lies in our unity. Whether success greets us or not, we stand together—as a family, unwavering and forever. Because beyond any exam or outcome, it's the journey, the love, and the resilience we shared that truly define us. And as for Yojan, with his unwavering hard work, resilience, and the life lessons carved from this JEE journey, we have no doubt—he will turn his dreams into reality.

Let The Journey Speak

As I close this book, I've made a conscious decision—not to reveal Yojan's final result or the name of the college he joins. Because this story isn't about a rank, a scorecard, or a college name. It's about the journey. The struggles, the breakthroughs, the late-night doubts, and the early morning resolve.

If I were to end with a rank or a college, some readers might subconsciously measure success by that yardstick. But every child is different. Every journey is unique. For some, success might be an IIT tag. For others, it could be discovering a passion, learning to rise after a fall, or simply completing the race with dignity.

So let this story end without a number. Let it remain open—like the future of every dreamer reading this. And let it remind us all that the journey, with all its highs and lows, is what truly shapes us.